A Thousand Stories for a Little Pianist

A Creative Approach to Developing Students' Imaginations

Based on the Russian School of Piano

Written and Illustrated by
Katrin Arefy

To my father,
who advises me with his silence and
supports me endlessly.

And to all the children of my country.

Katrin
January 2009
Berkeley, CA

Table of Contents

Part 1: The Teaching Philosophy

Part 2: Suggested Music Material

Part 1

The Teaching Philosophy

Prelude

This book is the expression of my deepest belief in music as a cultural tool and in children as the dearest treasure of any nation.

I am addressing talented young teachers who are starting their careers, as well as those teachers who never stop learning.

The best teachers I trained in my piano school are those who, in the job interview, told me: "I don't really use a specific method book. I just teach using my intuition." On the other hand, I recognize less creative teachers when I see they cannot change their old habit of going page by page through a book.

The music provided in part two of this book gives teachers some material and should be only a part of a teacher's ever-growing collection of music for students. Not all the pieces in part two are meant to be played by all students, and the order of the pieces is also subject to change based on each student's need.

As in all Russian methods of piano playing, in this book the student starts with the third finger, which is the pivot of the hand. In the Russian school of piano, we begin not with exercises, but with folk music. This allows the student to be immersed in meaningful music from the very first day.

Even though this book was designed for younger children, teachers can also apply these concepts and use the pieces in part two with their beginning teenage and adult students.

Acknowledgments

I was honored to receive not only advice and suggestions but also encouragement and support from my wonderful teacher, Irina Evgenievna Temchenko, during my time as a student in Moscow and later while working on this book. I am extremely grateful to her. I am also very thankful to Professor William Wellborn at the San Francisco Conservatory of Music for his invaluable suggestions and very thoughtful comments. My gratitude to my creative writing teacher, Andy Couturier, who knows the art of teaching, for all I have learned from him and for his feedback on the early drafts.

I am grateful to my friends who accompanied me throughout the completion of this work: to Kirill Mostov for being my inspiration; to Artin Der Minassians for being so generous with his knowledge and time in helping with every step of this project; to W. Ross Ayers for his professional advice and for being there when I needed him; to Irina Behrendt, Esfir Ross and Reza Irani for making some hard-to-find sources available to me; and to my dear Reza Rohani for his wise suggestions towards the end of this long journey.

I am grateful to those individuals who helped with the production of the book: to my assistant Gregory Armstrong for patiently helping with the final editing and meticulously caring about all details; to Janet Wagner for her thorough editing; to Arya Ghavamian for making the photos; to Hsuan Yang for the interior layout; to Scott Lambridis and the participants of his local creatives' monthly gatherings for their sincere help and support; and to Ryan Mintz and Mike Earles for proofreading.

Recognition to my students Azal Laal, Elaine Jutamulia, Nicolas Theunissen, Sam Kaplan-Pettus and Nikolas Nettesheim, whose compositions are the ornaments of this book. Many thanks also to their supportive parents.

The greatest appreciation goes to two people: Farzaneh Rafipour, my mother, for her big loving heart, and Sadegh Arefi, my father, for his intellectual mind and content soul. I am forever indebted for their never-ending love and care.

Artobolevskaya and What I Have Learned from Her

Without a doubt, Anna Artobolevskaya's[1] teaching philosophy has had the most profound impact on my professional career as a piano teacher and provides the foundation for this book. I started my teaching career using Artobolevskaya's book *First Meet with the Music*. Working with her book requires a very deep understanding of the Russian school of piano.

Artobolevskaya was an outstanding piano teacher at the Moscow Central Music School. She was known for her enthusiasm and endless creative approaches for each individual student. In the art of teaching the piano, Artobolevskaya was a supreme artist.

First Meet with the Music came into being in an organic way, arising from her teaching practice. For many years, Artobolevskaya had been making music notebooks for each of her students in class. She would explain the musical alphabet, rewrite the pieces that they chose, and then let them draw a picture for the piece. During the lesson they would make stories and lyrics for the pieces and give each piece a name. Each notebook looked different, depending on the student's age and personality. After years of teaching, there were many of these unique music notebooks. It took seven years for a publisher to make a book out of this treasure.

In her book, Artobolevskaya invites teachers to a continuous exploration throughout their careers. She believes in self-improvement for each individual student, and encourages teachers not to interfere with the natural growth of the musician.

She wrote in the preface of her book: "The first important duty of a teacher is to inspire the child so that he desires to learn and master the language of music. Indeed, to find the best approach and achieve the best result, those teachers who have spent their lives and energies teaching music to children should share their experiences and ideas with other teachers. This book was written for the sake of this goal."[2]

As a teacher, I learned constant searching from Artobolevskaya. I learned to believe in students and their abilities. Artobolevskaya gave me the golden key in the teaching process: love.

---

[1] Anna Artobolevskaya (1905-1988) was a pianist and outstanding teacher at Moscow Central Music School. Among her pupils were Rosa Tamarkina, Alexei Nasedkin, and Alexei Lubimov. Her brilliant talent as a teacher is reflected in her two books *First Meet with the Music* and *The Little Pianist's Repertoire*. She was a student of Maria Yudina.

[2] Anna Artobolevskaya, *First Meet with the Music* (Moscow: R.M.I, 1996), v.

Love Is the First Step

*"The opening is so crucial,
only crème de la crème should be allowed."*
- Josef Hofmann [3]

The musical seedling will be planted in a student's mind during the very first music lessons. Whether or not it grows to become a tree will be determined by the way it is imbedded.

The piano teacher's primary duty is to help the student love the music. What is our tool to help the student love the music? The music itself! Opening the door to the magical world of music and using understandable music that is age appropriate are the first steps on this path.

Colorful folk and children's songs are great materials to inspire students and show them that music has a story. Part two of this book provides a collection of colorful music appropriate for children. At first glance, some of the pieces might look difficult, but trust your students' abilities, and you will be surprised to see how they will make the effort to practice even the most challenging piece when they like it.

Stories, games, and toys are part of a child's daily life. Music teachers should bring the music into the child's world, rather than bringing the child into the music lesson. Kids should learn music through stories and games, without realizing that they are in a lesson. It is especially important not to scare away young students with something too serious, difficult, or boring.

Love of music is a contagious disease that can be transferred from the teacher to the student. The teacher should be able to become the student's friend from the very first lesson. If a student doesn't like the music teacher, you cannot expect him or her to like the lesson. Children are naïve; their minds are like clean pieces of paper, and everything you write on this paper will stay on it forever. Teachers must therefore be conscientious and tactful with every child starting music education. A music teacher who works with children needs to have many qualities in addition to being a good musician. Becoming the child's trusted friend, understanding his or her abilities, being creative in class, and nurturing the student's imagination are all impossible if the teacher doesn't love children and the music.

---

[3] Josef Hofmann (1876-1957) was a Polish pianist, pedagogue, and composer. He is considered one of the greatest pianists of his time.

What Is the Next Step?

Learning different piano skills does not necessarily go parallel with learning music theory.

For instance, when learning the theory of scales, one should start with C major, but Chopin believed that the C major scale is the hardest scale to play on the piano. He believed that playing those scales with five black keys are much easier than playing the C major because those scales require long fingers to be on the black keys and short fingers on the white keys. As a result, the hands will sit on the keys in their most natural shape.

The first and easiest technique on the piano is playing a non-legato melody with only the third fingers. For a beginning student, starting in a five-finger position can easily cause stiffness of the hands and no control over the sound. Instead, if the student plays a non-legato melody, with the third fingers dropping freely into the keys, listening to each sound played, the student has performed the first step of piano technique. This way of teaching has its roots in Chopin's school of piano playing.[4] Chopin would start his students with staccato, then introduce non-legato, and only later, legato.[5]

Fat   cat   fat fat cat.   Fat   cat   saw a   rat.

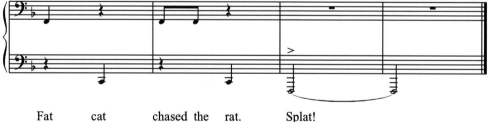

Fat   cat   chased the rat.   Splat!

Ex. 1. "Fat Cat"

Playing one note at a time, a student can control the sound and keep his or her hands relaxed. In this step, the student doesn't read the music but plays after looking at the teacher's hands.

---

[4] In his sketch of a method book that he never finished, Chopin refers to the third finger as "the middle and the pivot." See Jean-Jacques Eigeldinger, ed., *Chopin: Pianist and Teacher as Seen by His Students*, trans. Naomi Shohet, Krysia Osostowicz, and Roy Howat (Cambridge: Cambridge University Press, 2002), 195.

[5] See four steps of Chopin's exercise in Ibid., 33-34.

When playing with the third finger, the hand will freely dive into the key and sit on the third finger. The other fingers will lie lightly on other keys, and the hand will keep its natural shape. Students will feel the whole arm, from shoulder to third fingertip, sitting and lifting on the key as one unit and developing a relaxed wrist. This easiest technique on the piano is difficult enough to require at least a few lessons of practice on non-legato pieces and a lot of attention from both the teacher and the student.

Fig. 1. Student's hands playing with the third fingers

After this step, students will start using the other long fingers (second and fourth fingers), and later will try to connect two sounds together to make slurs. Legato playing is one of the hardest techniques on the piano. Therefore, very short legato phrases are recommended to begin learning this skill.

Ex. 2. "Étude" by Elena Gnessina[6]
This is a good piece to start practicing legato with the second and third fingers. Encouraging the student to create lyrics for the piece will help him or her easily understand the idea of question and answer in this piece.

The next challenge will be listening to both hands play at the same time and balancing the sounds so that the melody sings while the accompaniment stays in the background. To work on this skill, the student will practice easy pieces in which the melody is played with one hand and the accompaniment with the other hand. The only way to balance the sounds is for the student to listen to them.

Ex. 3. Russian Folk Song
Here the student plays a harmonic fifth interval with the left hand and learns the theory of intervals as well. There are more examples of easy accompaniment in part two of this book.

[6] Elena Gnessina (1874-1967) was a Russian pianist and pedagogue. She and her sisters founded the Gnessin School of Music in Moscow, where she was the director (1944-53) and piano professor. She studied with Vasily Safonov and Ferruccio Busoni. Among her students were Lev Oborin and Aram Khachaturian. She is the author of *Piano Alphabet*.

Students should always work on understanding the artistic image of the piece. As the student moves on, the stories and meanings of the pieces become more complex and deeper. Teachers should choose the pieces according to the student's maturity and ability to understand the content. Many pieces with easy note-reading are not appropriate for an immature and inexperienced student because the profound meaning of the pieces simply requires more life experience. Giving Beethoven's last "Bagatelles" (op. 119 or op. 126) to a seven-year-old is like reading Goethe's shorter prose narratives to a child.

There is a vast music literature written by masters for children. Great composers from J.S. Bach to Clementi, Schumann, Tchaikovsky, Bartók, Kabalevsky, Prokofiev, and others have created wonderful pieces that are appropriate for younger ages.

Ex. 4. "Winter" by M. Krutitsky

Despite the slow tempo and fairly easy note-reading, this deeply sad music may be too dark for some children to tolerate or sometimes to feel. The teacher should carefully decide when the student is ready to practice this piece.

Ex. 5. "The Bear" by German Galynin
Younger students will learn this tricky rhythm and articulation easily because they love the
image of the bear stomping in this piece.

In this way of teaching, pieces are not introduced based on a student's knowledge of theory;
instead, students will learn theory based on the piece on which they're working. The teacher
will introduce the new theory subject of the piece in a creative story or game. Thus, the first
pieces are not limited to the key of C major or the first and small octaves.

For example, in Artobolevskaya's arrangement of the motif from Franz Liszt's Hungarian
Rhapsody no. 2 (ex. 6) the student learns the black key B flat. In Liakhovitskaya's "Étude"
(ex. 7) the student learns about intervals. The best piece to start learning triads is on
Knipper's piece (ex. 8) because all triads are in root position.

Ex. 6. "Hopscotch"
This is one of the first pieces in Artobolevskaya's book. Here the student doesn't read the
music, but plays after looking at the teacher's hands.

Ex. 7. "Étude" by Sofia Liakhovitskaya

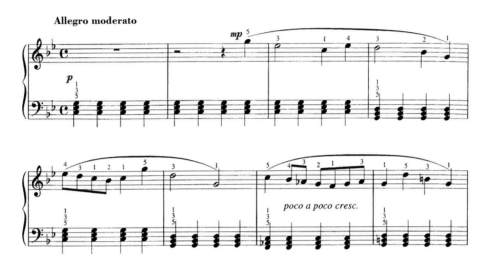

Ex. 8. "Open Fields, Boundless Plains" by Lev Knipper

Even though the chapters in part two were designed based on pianistic difficulties, there is no required order for the pieces within each chapter. In fact, it is very important to choose only as many pieces as the student needs from each chapter and work on them in the order that is defined by the student's abilities, age, and interest, because each child is unique.

Having no set order for the pieces does not mean that it is not important which piece comes next. Quite the contrary; it is absolutely crucial which piece comes next for each and every single student, and that is why it should be chosen very carefully by teacher and student together.

A curriculum guideline helps teachers keep track of what theory and technique subjects they have taught and what still needs to be covered. Having a curriculum allows the student to arrange his or her repertoire from a wide library without missing any theory, technique, or ear-training subject on the way.

A sample curriculum guideline is provided on page 44. The curriculum can be continually revised and developed in each teacher's studio.

The Meaning of the Music

Even a very young child can understand the story of an easy children's song. A young student can tell if the music is a dance, a song, or a musical story and if it is happy or sad, funny or serious, rainy or sunny, or red or blue.

Music always has a story to tell, even if this story is purely musical. Students start interpreting the very easy short pieces that they practice using words, drawings, movements, and mimics. This is what we call *story making* for the musical piece.

The first step on the path of recreating the musical piece is understanding its meaning. All the tools that a pianist uses in the process of shaping this story are called *technique.* Working on technique is pointless if it is not based on the meaning of the music. Technique is nothing but the ability to embody the artistic image in sound. Heinrich Neuhaus[7] wrote in his book *The Art of Piano Playing*: "I often tell my pupils that the word 'technique' comes from the Greek word *techne* and that *techne* means art. Any improvement of technique is an improvement of art itself." He goes on to say:

> Work on the artistic image should begin at the very first stage of learning the piano and note-reading. By this I mean that if a child is able to reproduce some very simple melody, it is essential to make this first 'performance' expressive, in other words, that the nature of the performance should correspond to the nature (the 'content') of the melody; for this purpose, it is especially advisable to use folk tunes in which the emotional and poetic element is much more apparent than even in the best educational compositions for children.[8]

Unfortunately in many cases, especially in the beginning steps, piano lessons turn into typing class. In these classes students learn to press the right keys and count for rhythm, but it takes months before they will hear any music in their music class!

In most piano method books, each lesson is designed to teach a certain subject in the musical alphabet or in theory (e.g., a new note, rhythm value, or dynamic sign). What is sorely missing in these kinds of books is the musical image. One can hardly even call the material they offer in these books music.[9]

Having a variety of colors and characters in pieces can help the student's creativity and imagination to flourish. For example, one image for Artobolevskaya's arrangement of Liszt

---

[7] Heinrich Neuhaus (1888-1964) was a genius pianist, teacher, professor, and the director of the Moscow Conservatory. Among his pupils were Emil Gilels and Sviatoslav Richter.

[8] Heinrich Neuhaus, *The Art of Piano Playing*, trans. K.A. Leibovitch (London: Kahn & Averill, 1993), 2.

[9] Most of the piano method books I've seen postponed introducing key signatures for as long as possible. As a result the book is either too monotonous (all pieces are in C major), or if there is a piece in F major, it appears with no key signature.

(ex. 6, page 16) can be a boy jumping, so the accents on the dotted eighth notes can be the jumps. He is jumping pretty fast—*vivace*. Or the Tatar folk music (ex. 9) can be a little bird picking up food; fingertips that actively move to make staccato notes can demonstrate the bird's beak. In *Lullaby* by Philipp (ex. 10), the right hand can be the mommy bear singing the song, and the left hand can be the bee with his legs stuck in the honey saying "heeeelp!" so softly that almost nobody can hear him.

Ex. 9. Tatar Folk Song

Ex. 10. "Lullaby" by Isidor Philipp

Creativity

A teacher-storyteller will nurture a student-story maker. Teaching by using stories, images, and metaphors can inspire students and cultivate their creative minds. This creative mind is essential to recreate the musical piece from notes on the paper to the music that communicates to an audience.

Only the music that has something to say can give the teacher and the student a chance for this artistic process. That is why in this book we begin with folk music and continue with the original music of great composers.

Music, which was once written by a composer, will live a new life each and every time it is in the pianist's hands. Aldo Ciccolini[10], in an interview with *International Piano* magazine, says: "I try to tell a story but never the same story for the same piece. The audience doesn't know the story I'm telling, but they know I'm telling a story."[11]

If you take this storytelling away from the pianist, there will be nothing left but a typist. And if you take away the creative element from your piano lesson, you cannot claim that you taught music.

---

[10] Aldo Ciccolini (1925 -) is a brilliant Italian pianist and professor at the Paris Conservatory.

[11] Joe Laredo, "All in the Imagination" (an interview with Aldo Ciccolini), *International Piano* 57 (2005): 14.

Each Student Is Unique

Each student is so different and unique that it is impossible to have one method book and lesson plan for all students. Using one book and going through it page by page like a *musician-making machine* will kill the student's uniqueness on the spot.

Marguerite Long[12] writes in her book *Piano*: "I don't believe in dogmatism in piano. As some doctors believe 'medicine doesn't exist, only the patient exists,' I want to take the risk and say a method doesn't exist, only the student exists."[13]

In my lessons, each student has a binder. We choose the new piece together during a lesson and add it to the binder. I choose a few pieces and play them for the student, but the student decides which piece to play because that is the one he or she can relate to better.

Thus, no two binders are the same. From the first lesson, when the student chooses seven animals for seven octaves, the binder is already showing his or her unique choices. Then, when selecting pieces, students make stories for the new piece, name the piece, and draw a picture based on it. In this way, while working on the meaning of the piece, students will have a chance to express their creativity, and the teacher will have a chance to see the students' inner worlds.

Choosing the new piece, choosing a name for the piece, discovering the story of the piece, and even choosing finger numbers are all the student's job in class.

Students are different not only in their characters and inner worlds, but also in the way they learn. It is the teacher's responsibility to find the weak and strong points in each student and help each accordingly.

For instance, if a student plays a piece by memory immediately and doesn't look at the notes very often, we spend more time on sight-reading and note-reading. With those who can hardly even sing a simple short melody, we play different games to work on ear training. With Nicolas, a very intelligent boy who says, "I don't want to practice other people's music, I want to play my own," I use any opportunity in class to talk more about musical theory, scales, and chords. The piece "Bears Wobbling" on page 123 of this book is his composition, written by a six-year-old student who learns music in his own way.

---

[12] Marguerite Long (1874-1966) was a French pianist and professor at the Paris Conservatory from 1920-1946. Composers like Maurice Ravel, Darius Milhaud, and Gabriel Fauré dedicated their music to her.

[13] Marguerite Long, *Piano* (Paris: Salabert, c. 1959), quoted in Sofia Khentova, *Marguerite Long* (Moscow: Muzgyz, 1961), 54.

Invisible Teacher

"If my thought doesn't allow your thinking to go beyond it,
I will be ashamed of my thought."
- Manuchehr Jamali [14]

A mechanical way of teaching delivers knowledge to students, but an artistic way of teaching helps students find their own path.

In class with a teacher-artist, a student becomes curious and discovers a lot in music. The invisible teacher is beside the student, offering tips and explanations for each corner that attracts the student's attention.

Teacher-artists believe in students' abilities, can see their unique qualities, and help nurture students' imaginations. Teacher-artists set aside their "self" to let the student's "self" grow. They always employ the power of encouragement and allow the student's imagination to go beyond the teacher's thoughts.

[14] Manuchehr Jamali (1929-) is a modern-day Iranian philosopher. The quote is from the cover of his book *Bodies Are Too Heavy to Burden* (London: Kurmali Press, n.d.).

Story Time: Games and Stories

Each creative teacher has different games and stories to teach certain theory subjects or techniques, and experienced teachers know that one game or story doesn't necessarily work for all students. Here are some examples that I use in my class.

Piano as Another Toy: Introducing the Mechanism of the Piano

The piano's mechanism is beautiful, and knowing it helps the student understand how to work with the instrument. While explaining and showing its mechanism to the student with simple words, the teacher can focus the child's attention on the fact that pushing the keys down doesn't help make it sound better or that holding the damper pedal down will let all the strings sing, even those that we don't want!

After I show the student how the hammers touch the strings to make sound, and how the dampers hold them to make silence, I ask the student to make sound and silence on the piano and make short sounds and long sounds.

During the first lesson, the teacher is a stranger to the young student, and the piano might look like a big black box to the child. It is imperative to help the student look at the piano as a toy and the teacher as a friend. Opening the piano's lid, and showing the student the beautiful strings and the beautiful movement of hammers and dampers when the keys are played is a good way to start the first lesson.

The Story of Magical Flowers: Playing with the Hand's Weight

All my students, from children to adults, have heard this story that was inspired by a similar story from Yudovina-Galperina.[15]

In this story a pianist has an imaginary lake on his back. From this lake water will pour, and if the shoulders are not stiff, the water will pour to the arms, and from the arms to the forearms and wrists. If the wrists are soft and relaxed, water will go to the fingers, then the fingertips will sit on the keys, letting the water go to the keys. From the keys, water will go to the hammers, and when the hammers touch the strings, water will go to the strings. The strings will become magic flowers and start singing.

---

[15] See Tatyana Yudovina-Galperina, *At the Piano without Tears* (Saint Petersburg: Saint Petersburg Union Artists Enterprise, 1996), 70.

This image that beautifully pictures the connection between the touch and the piano's sound is very helpful not only for younger children, but also for music students at university level. This metaphor shows that piano playing doesn't happen merely between the pianist's fingers and keys; rather, it starts from the pianist's back and goes all the way to the piano's strings.

Seven Octaves, Seven Animals: Introducing the Octaves

Animals' characters are very attractive to children, and I use them a lot to inspire children's imaginations. In the beginning, the child will recognize the seven octaves on the piano, associating them with seven animals that he or she chooses. There are many pieces in part two to demonstrate how each register can sound like an animal. Little by little, the student will learn the real name of each octave, but in the beginning, animals help them remember high and low voices, and up and down on the keyboard. For example, I use "The Bear" (ex. 5, page 16) to show that the bear has a low voice and that he lives down on the keyboard, and "Birds" (ex. 11) to show the high voice and birds living up on the tree. Understanding this concept helps make note-reading easier later on. The simple fact that when the note goes one up on the staff, you play the next key up on the keyboard can be very confusing for students if they don't have a clear image of up and down on the keyboard in their mind.

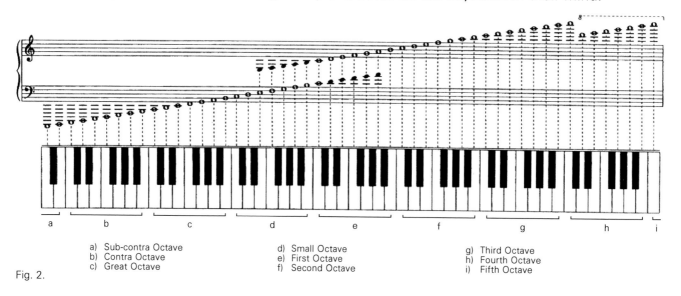

a) Sub-contra Octave
b) Contra Octave
c) Great Octave
d) Small Octave
e) First Octave
f) Second Octave
g) Third Octave
h) Fourth Octave
i) Fifth Octave

Fig. 2.

The Story of Two Sisters and Three Brothers: Introducing the Keyboard

One of the problems with beginning students is that to name any key, they count the keys in order instead of recognizing each key by itself. To avoid that, the keys should be introduced not in order but randomly. For example, D is between the two black keys, B is on top of three black keys, and so on.

Ex. 11. "Birds" by Avrelian Rubakh

Creative teachers will make many different stories to teach the keys. Here is my example: The two black keys are two sisters, and the three black keys are three brothers. The seven white keys in an octave are seven gardens in a house. Before naming the white keys I will make sure that the student can easily recognize the brothers and sisters on the piano. Then they see how the two sisters share a garden and name it garden D, the younger and middle brother share garden G, the older brother has the B garden, which he doesn't share with anybody, and so on.

Which key to introduce first depends on which song the student is going to play. I usually start with D and G for "Owl Song" (ex. 12).

Ex. 12. "Owl Song"

This piece is for the playing-by-ear period when students will be learning the names of the keys. Students learn this song not by reading the music but by playing after looking at the teacher's hands.

Students learn the seven white keys on the piano and choose seven colors for them. These seven colors, which will be used later in note-reading, help younger children remember the notes more easily. When the student and not the teacher chooses the color, the student remembers it with no effort.

To teach the black keys, which students learn after only a few lessons, I tell them a story about a butterfly that flies down from garden B and sits on the older brother's head. The older brother's name becomes B flat. In a similar story a bug will fly from garden F, going up to sit on the younger brother's head, so his name becomes F sharp.

The teacher's ability to make these stories interesting will help the student to easily remember them forever.

The Story of the Musical Family: Rhythm Value

Rhythm value has to do with time. I have a story to picture the different duration of each note. In this story, different members of a family are walking the same distance to get to the house's door. Grandmother, who cannot walk very fast, is the whole note. It takes a long time for her to get to the door. We take our hands and clap and count for her: "one and two and three and four and." We clap while saying the numbers and open our hands while saying "and." The mother walks a little faster, and she is a dotted half note. The dot can be her shopping bag that makes her walk slower than father. We count for mother: "one and two and three and." The father walks fast as a half note, and the student is a quarter note: "one and." The eighth note in this story is a cat, which is the fastest one in the house. The cat just jumps to the door as we count: "one!"

Fig. 3.

While drawing the grandma and writing the note I ask the student, "How long does it take for grandma to get to the door? Take your hands and clap for her," then we clap and count together: 1 & 2 & 3 & 4 &.

The student learns all these rhythm values in one lesson, and doing some games helps him or her to remember them.

In a similar story, I introduce the rests. The point here is to show the student that the rest is a sign for silence and not a sign to stop the music. A rest has its own meaning in the musical story, each time taking a different personality. The musical story flows in sounds and rests.

The Story of the Two Kingdoms: Grand Staff

In this story, the top staff with the treble clef is a country. I start with counting the five lines and four spaces on it. I write line notes and space notes and tell the student that these are people who live on or in between the lines. I have the student write a few line notes and space notes. Before putting the treble clef on the staff, I tell the student that these people have a funny problem: They don't have names! So, they choose the smartest girl in the country to become their queen and to give them names. They call her Queen G. She lives on the second line, and she names any person who also lives on the second line after her: G.

In a similar story, I introduce King F (F clef) on the bottom staff, and the F note on the fourth line. King F and Queen G are good friends, and together make the grand staff. In this story, Middle C is a soldier who lives between the two countries. In this way, students learn the grand staff at once and not the two staves separately.

So far the student has learned three notes on the staff (F, C, and G). Which note he or she learns next depends on which song the student chooses to play. After learning a new note on the staff, the student finds its place on the piano.

Coloring the Notes: Making Note Reading Easy

Unlike most beginner books, this book doesn't start with the five-finger position. Students need to really know how to read the notes in order to play these colorful pieces that aren't stuck in five keys. In addition to practicing how to read the notes in weekly reading exercises and sight-reading exercises, I make practicing the pieces easier by coloring the notes.

The student has already chosen the colors for the seven keys; now he or she learns the notes using the same seven colors. To do this, I use a diagram of a staff and keyboard that links each note on the staff to its appropriate key on the keyboard (see page 28). First I ask the student to find the note on the staff. Then I ask him or her to trace the line down to find where this note lives on the keys, and we color the note (person) the same as its key (garden).

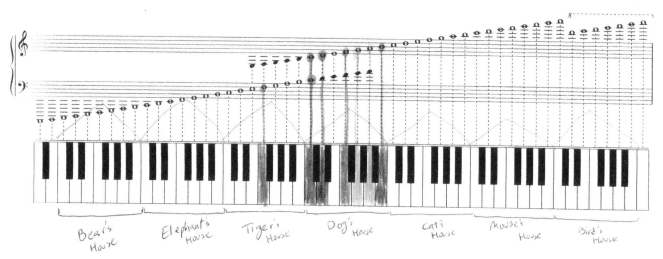

Fig. 4.

In this way, we can keep track of which notes the child knows and which he or she should learn next. Students learn the notes randomly in order to avoid counting the lines and spaces and to make note-reading faster.

When learning each new piece, the student first colors the notes. Coloring allows the student to play pieces with more difficult note reading in the early stages. This way, the challenge of note-reading doesn't stop them from learning new piano skills.

Here is an example from a student's binder:

Fig. 5.

Students should gradually get rid of colors as soon as they are ready. Even for the very new beginners, there is no need to color those notes that they can recognize easily.

For note reading exercises and easy sight-readings, we don't color the notes, so as to prepare the student for reading the notes without colors. Here is an example for one of the note reading exercises that the teacher writes in each lesson:

Fig. 6.

In these weekly exercises, students practice naming the notes. The teacher writes the exercise in each lesson to tailor it to the student's knowledge and need.

Naming the Piece, Drawing, and Making a Story: Bringing Out the Meaning of the Music

After the student chooses a new piece from the few that the teacher plays, he or she makes up a story for the piece and gives it a name. Spending a few minutes in class to draw a picture for the piece can give the student some creative time to express what he or she has heard in the music.

For some pieces it is easy to make lyrics in class. Lyrics will not only help to express the meaning of the music, but also help students practice on the rhythm.

Playing-by-Ear Period

In this step, students will learn a few short pieces by listening and looking at the teacher's hands. During this period the teacher's goal is to shape the student's hands and work on relaxation of the hands. Students learn how to let their third finger sit on the key or, as Artobolevskaya says, "dive into the key" and listen to the piano's response without getting distracted by note-reading.

Playing without the notes helps the students to develop their ear-training and musical memory. Students learn the piece in class in a way that they can remember and play at home.

How long should students stay in the playing-by-ear period? It depends on their age and learning abilities. A four-year-old might need five or six songs; a fast-learning six-year-old may need only two or three songs before he or she can play while looking at the notes. So, when a student has learned the keys on the piano, has more or less relaxed hands, can recognize at least five or six notes on the staff and the rhythm values easily, then it is time to have the student practice while looking at the notes.

The following exercise in the playing-by-ear period pursues the basic technique of dropping the free hand into the key and lifting it from the elbow: I ask the student to let his or her third finger sit on a key, let's say G, in the fourth octave. Of course, the student knows the fourth octave as an animal's house that he or she chose (see the story of seven octaves, seven animals on page 24). Then I tell the student to imagine that his or her hand is a bird. Let the bird sit on the garden G and rest there, listening to the piano's sound until it fades away and dies completely. Then, fly and sit on the G in the next house down (third octave), and so on.

This exercise that develops full-arm motion aims to achieve three important goals: 1. Finding and recognizing the keys on the piano; 2. Dropping and lifting on the keys with the third finger; and 3. Listening to the piano's response.

For children, this exercise is the story of a little bird that says hello to all animals every morning.

The "Owl Song" (ex. 12, page 25) is a good piece to start with in the playing-by-ear period. Recognizing gardens D and G is easy. This simple melody for third fingers lets the student cross one hand over the other. While crossing, there is no chance of stiffening the hand.

Playing While Looking at the Notes

When teaching the musical alphabet, it is important not to scare the student with its difficulties. No matter how you introduce note-reading, it should sound like an amazing and fun game! There are some examples in the Games and Stories chapter, but creative teachers can improvise many games and stories in the moment to perform their pedagogical goal.

Even though learning musical staves and rhythm values starts during the first lesson, students will start playing while looking at the notes after a few lessons. Teachers will know the timing is right when students have learned to play with the third fingers and relaxed hands, and their knowledge of notes is good enough that having the notes in front of them doesn't distract them from listening to the sound and relaxing their hands.

The first pieces that a student plays while looking at the notes are short non-legato phrases from folk songs or familiar children's songs arranged for third fingers only. In my class the student chooses one piece among the few that I play; then we make up a story for the piece and give it a name. We spend a few minutes drawing a picture about the song in the lesson. We clap the rhythm and read or color the notes, and then we play the piece while reading the notes.

In the example below, my four-year-old student named this song "A Blue Song" and drew a boy painting with the color blue.

Fig. 7. From a four-year-old student's binder

Playing with third fingers helps the beginning student develop a relaxed wrist. Coloring the notes makes the note-reading easier.

Little by little, students will no longer need to color the notes. This process should happen smoothly so that students don't even notice that their helpful colors are leaving them forever.

In most of the short pieces at the beginning of this book, there are no tempos or dynamic signs, and students get to choose those based on their own story for the piece. In this way, they will clearly understand that the tempo and dynamics come from the story of the piece.

Sight-reading and note-reading are activities that happen every lesson and every day at home. It is sometimes more challenging to make these exercises fun. To make it less dry and captivate the students, I use different games and toys. For example, I have the student time me as I tell the names of the notes in the exercise, and then I time her or him. This is a simple and fun game for those who are competitive. I also use a whiteboard and colored markers to create matching games that help students learn theory during their lessons. It's amazing how simple games on the board with colored markers can turn a dry topic like theory into the part of the lesson that students look forward to the most.

For sight-reading, a student can start with a few easy notes that the teacher writes in a short phrase based on the student's current knowledge of notes, and continue with any easy book available elsewhere. I would choose a variety of books instead of sticking with one.

Shaping the Student's Hands

A student's hands are like clay, and they should be shaped by the teacher's hands, little by little, as they are working together. Shaping a student's hands starts during the first lesson, when the student first touches the keys.

Different stories and metaphors can help the student understand how to put his or her hands on the piano, but the best way is to hold the student's hands and literally shape them so that the wrist is relaxed, the arms don't become glued to his or her body, the shoulders drop, and the fingertips actively dive to the end of the keys.

Fig. 8. The teacher shaping the student's hands

Artobolevskaya would say to the young student: "Give me your hand. Let your hand be mine for a minute."[16] Then she would take the student's forearm and turn it back and forth very quickly as if preparing bread dough. The child would laugh, watching his fingers turn so fast, it looked like he had ten fingers on each hand. Only after his forearm and arm were free and relaxed would Artobolevskaya put the student's third fingertip on the key in a way that his hand kept its natural shape.

---

[16] Anna Artobolevskaya, *First Meet with the Music* (Moscow: R.M.I, 1996), XI.

Fig. 9. Making bread dough

For the first few pieces, students play with the third finger only; this way, the student can feel his or her whole hand, from shoulder to third fingertip, as one unit. This lets the student work on the first and most important technique on the piano, which is dropping onto and lifting off from one key.

Fig. 10. The student's hand dropping onto the key

Fig. 11. The student's hand lifting up from the key

I don't use the phrase "curve your fingers" in my classes because the wrong image of curved fingers can lead the student to adopt an unnatural hand shape. Instead, I show the student that each finger has imaginary lips on the fingertips and when the student plays the piano, the finger's lips will kiss the keys. This metaphor not only helps the student to shape his or her hand, but it also creates the image that the piano is alive.

Artobolevskaya uses a pencil with an eraser to show this metaphor. The elastic quality of the eraser is different from the plain wooden pencil. The fingers kiss the eraser one by one and the student feels his or her fingertips.

In this way, while shaping students' hands, you can remind them that each finger is like a little person and has qualities that are different from other fingers. We should treat the piano as if it were alive. The piano's response, its sound, depends on our fingers' approach and behavior.

Fig. 12. The student's fingers kissing an eraser

Let the Piano Sing: Working on the Sound from the First Steps

If a painter's material is color, a pianist's material is sound. Working on the sound is ongoing work for a pianist.

Having the student listen to the sound that he or she produces will be easier if it happens during the first steps of piano playing. If postponed, it will require a lot of effort from the student and the teacher to build the student's sensitivity to the sound.

Even young children can distinguish a good quality sound from a bad one. Just let them hear a phrase once in a hammering sound and then in a nice singing tone. They will definitely tell you which one was bad.

Making a beautiful tone is directly connected to the touch. Teachers should invite the student's attention to the sound quality by explaining how the instrument will scream if you bang on it and how it will sing if you grab the key with a sensitive fingertip and deep touch.

During the first lesson, students can experience how the higher sounds on the piano die faster and the lower sounds will sing for a long time. This can be their first experiment in listening to the piano's response.

Later, when working on the pieces, the story of the piece will show the student what character the sound should have. For example, in "Bears Wobbling" (page 123) the left hand is the bear stomping; in "The Rainbow" (page 81) the image of the long curved beautiful line of a rainbow helps the student overcome the challenge of playing a legato melody line divided between the two hands; in "Tatar Folk Song" (page 70) the staccato sounds like little birds chirping. The staccato sound in "Tatar Folk Song" is finger staccato, which is totally different from the clumsy and heavy staccato in "This is a Funny Way to Dance" (page 135), or the soft and puffy staccato on the left hand in "This is Our Garden" (page 137).

In the Beginning There Was Rhythm:
A Few Words on Rhythm

Anna Artobolevskaya said: "Rhythm is not something to teach, it is something to transmit. The first three fundamentals to get the rhythm are the ears, musical memory and the physical feeling of movement. Children experience rhythm while being swung to a lullaby and later in a swing and by pedaling a bike. All these help children to feel the pulse in rhythmic movements."[17]

The best way to learn rhythm is through rhythmic body movements. For young children, it can be clapping or marching; for older ones it can be conducting movements. With the music provided in "I Can Play a Song" in part two of this book, children will listen, sing, and clap the song a few times to get the rhythm before they play it. Problems with rhythm should be addressed and solved separately from all other difficulties.

Here are some examples of common rhythm issues:

Switching triple and quadruple rhythms around is a common mistake, even in the more advanced levels. Matching words with the rhythm and singing it will solve this problem very quickly. I use this tool not only for beginners but also for my advanced students.

With one student who changed the $\frac{6}{8}$ time to $\frac{2}{4}$ in "Clowning" by Dmitry Kabalevsky (ex. 13), we sang her mother's name, Tali'eh, dividing it into three syllables (Ta-li-eh), and she started to play the rhythm correctly right away.

In longer pieces and especially with sonata forms, another issue is keeping the tempo steady. In this case, I ask the student to conduct the whole piece as though conducting an imaginary pianist. In this way, a student can solve the tempo problem apart from all other difficulties and feel the piece as a unified whole in one constant tempo.

Ex. 13. "Clowning" by Kabalevsky

---

[17] Anna Artobolevskaya, *First Meet with the Music* (Moscow: R.M.I, 1996), XX.

Ex. 14. The same piece the way the student used to play it

Metronome is Metric, Not Rhythmic

A metronome is a tool to measure the meter. Rhythm is like the human body's pulse or a river's waves, and not the mechanical tick-tock of a clock or a metronome.

Practicing with the metronome is an attempt to match the music with a mechanical sound that exists outside of a student's mind and outside of the music. This approach, even if it succeeds, cannot enrich the music or the student's mind; it only causes mechanical playing.

Discovering the Pedal

A pianist should play the pedal not with his feet but with his ears!

Very often my young students point at the pedals during an early lesson and ask me, "What are these?" I simply explain the mechanism of each pedal, showing how each one gives a different color to the piano's sound.

To explain the damper pedal to a child, I start with a fun experience. I open the piano's lid and ask the student to watch the strings while I push the pedal down. After the dampers lift up from the strings, I ask the student to say something loudly while facing the strings. The strings resonate with the sound, and it is fascinating to the child. Then we have the same experience using the piano's sound. The student pushes the damper pedal and, while holding it down, plays a key on the piano and hears how all the other strings make a little sound too. I show the student that if we want only one key to sing, we need to play the key first and then hold the sound with the damper pedal. The student plays and compares these two ways of pedaling.

Pushing the left pedal on the grand piano and watching how all the keys move is also amusing to children. Almost all of them ask, "Why are the keys moving?" I show them that the keys and hammers move together so that when you play a key the hammers touch only two strings instead of three. These two strings sing normally, but since the damper is not holding the third string, it whispers in secret. Then we listen to the magical sound of playing with the left pedal.

The middle pedal on the grand piano is a total surprise for the child. The experience of holding some sounds on the pedal and having the rest of the keys act without the pedal's effect is almost like magic.

Even though the young child still has a long way to go before he or she starts playing with the pedal in the pieces, explaining the mechanism of the pedals enriches the child's imagination. Noticing the different colors that the pedals produce helps the student develop his or her ears' sensitivity.

Later, when the student has developed enough skills to listen and control the sound, he or she can start playing pieces with the pedal. After getting a basic understanding of the syncopation pedal and rhythmic pedal, students need to understand that pedaling is for different purposes. Pedaling can be for the sake of harmony, to make the sounds legato, or to make a different color and timbre. Very often, pedaling can be for a combination of the above reasons.

To find out the right way of pedaling in each piece, again we start with the image and the story behind the music.

Here are some examples of pieces with the damper pedal:

Rhythmic Pedal

This is when the pedal is pressed down right at the same time as the note(s). For example, in "Varan Varane" (ex. 15) each chord on the left hand can be played with the rhythmic pedal. This way of pedaling will make the chords sound more rich and smooth.

Ex. 15. "Varan Varane," a Kurdish folk song

As another example, "The Playful Pony" (page 128) can be played with rhythmic pedal on the first chord of each measure to emphasize the pulse of the music and make the sound less dry.

Shorter Rhythmic Pedal (Pedal Staccato)

This very short and sharp rhythmic pedal gives the sound a richer or stronger effect. Using staccato pedal on the first beat of each measure in "This is Our Garden" (page 137) will make the left hand sound more smooth and puffy like the sound of a timpani played softly.

Syncopation Pedal

This way of pedaling is the most common one and can be used for holding the harmony, or making a legato line. Béla Bartók[18] very clearly explains the syncopation pedal in the notes as seen below.

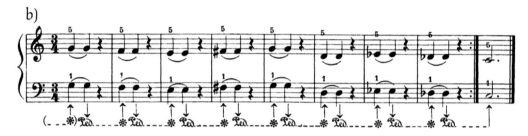

Ex. 16. A pedal exercise by Béla Bartók

Many pieces in the last two chapters of this book can be played with syncopation pedal. "Mexican Folk Song" (page 125) can be a good piece to start learning syncopation pedal. Here the pedal should be pressed down after the first chord of each measure, even in the measures with tied notes in the left hand.

[18] Béla Bartók (1881-1945) was a Hungarian composer, pianist, and ethnomusicologist.

Music for All Children

"Music should be taught to everybody,
in any form and to any level,
but training to become a professional musician
should be given only to very few."
- Alexander Goldenweiser [19]

Music as a cultural tool has always been the essential education for any progressive society. When music is not part of a school's program, private music teachers fill the gap, taking on a huge responsibility.

In his book *The Art of Piano Playing*, Heinrich Neuhaus says the duty of the music teacher is "not merely to teach the student how to play well," but also "to make the student more intelligent, more perceptive, more honest, more just, more determined...."[20] Having this duty on their shoulders, music teachers cannot choose only musically gifted children, because music is for all children.

I believe in music education as a key to the cultural development of any nation. The difference between societies in which people listen to good music, the kind of music that can widen and cultivate a person's mind, and those in which people don't have the habit and appreciation of listening to good music proves my belief. This huge cultural evolution starts from children's music education.

Giving a child the gift of musical education is opening the door of music not only to the child but also to a family. Each child who knocks on your door is a tiny, vulnerable plant looking for a loving cultivator. The future of your society starts with those little children.

[19] Alexander Goldenweiser (1875-1961) was a Russian pianist, composer, author, and professor at Moscow Conservatory. Among his pupils were Dmitry Kabalevsky and Tatyana Nikolayeva.

[20] Heinrich Neuhaus, *The Art of Piano Playing* (Moscow: Muzika, 1987), 29.

Sample Curriculum Guidelines

Level 1

Repertoire

- Play simple non-legato pieces using the third fingers after watching the teacher's hands.
- Play pieces using the second, third, and fourth fingers one hand at a time while looking at the notes (use colors if necessary).
- Understand the phrasing of the pieces.
- Understand the meaning of the music by creating a story for each piece and naming it.

Theory and Ear Training

- Recognize the keys on the piano, including sharps and flats and names of the octaves.
- Be able to sing a small interval after hearing it played on the piano. Students should also recognize if the interval is going up or down by listening to it.
- Recognize the dynamic signs: *p, f, mf, mp.*
- Recognize and read at least twelve notes on the staff (from F on the small octave to C on the first octave).
- Understand and count rhythm values: whole, half, dotted half, quarter and eighth notes.
- Recognize minor and major pieces by ear.
- Be able to write line notes and space notes.
- Understand up and down on the piano and on the staff.
- Be able to repeat a rhythm by clapping or playing on one key.
- Understand time signatures: $\frac{2}{4}$, $\frac{3}{4}$ and $\frac{4}{4}$.

Technique

- Achieve relaxation of the hands.
- Be able to drop and lift the hand on the third finger.
- Be able to make a slur using the third and second fingers.
- Be aware of the piano's response to the touch.
- Be able to listen to the sound and rests accurately.

Sight-reading

- Sight-read simple rhythm exercises in $\frac{2}{4}$, $\frac{3}{4}$ and $\frac{4}{4}$ time signatures.
- Sight-read easy pieces of two or three different notes (written by the teacher) and sight-read books as easy as *A Dozen A Day Mini Book* by Edna-Mae Burnam.

Listening Suggestions

- *First Meet with the Music* by Anna Artobolevskaya. To be played by teacher in class.
- *Peter and the Wolf* by Sergei Prokofiev.

Level 2

Repertoire
- Play simple pieces with legato, staccato, and portato, playing with both hands at the same time (learned from the notes and memorized).
- Name the pieces and make a story for each one.
- Play one piece from Bartók's *Mikrokosmos* vol. 1 (to learn five-finger position).

Theory and Ear Training
- Recognize famous tempo signs: allegro, moderato, andante.
- Recognize and read ten more notes on the staff (from B on the great octave to G on the second octave).
- Recognize major second, major third, perfect fourth and perfect fifth intervals on the staff and by ear.
- Be able to sing a melodic interval after hearing it played harmonic (major second, major third, perfect fourth, perfect fifth).
- Be able to write second, third, fourth, and fifth melodic and harmonic intervals on the staff.
- Understand the dotted quarter note in written exercises and playing.
- Be able to repeat a three-note phrase on the piano by ear and transpose it.
- Understand and be able to improvise question and answer phrases (in C major).
- Understand time signatures: $\frac{3}{8}$ and $\frac{6}{8}$

Technique
- Shape the hands and fingers.
- Play finger staccato.
- Play two or three notes legato.

Sight-reading
- Sight-read any easy music available.

Listening Suggestions
- Camille Saint-Saëns, *Carnival of the Animals*.
- Francis Poulenc, *The Story of Babar, the Little Elephant*.

Reference List for Music Examples in Part One

Part 2

Suggested Music Material

I Can Play a Song

*Playing While Looking at the
Teacher's Hands*

Here are a few songs for you to practice playing with your longer fingers, the second, third and fourth fingers. While playing, make sure your forearm and wrist are smooth and soft. You don't have to read the music to learn these pieces. But make sure you learn the name of all the white and black keys.

Listen to your teacher play the song, clap and sing it, and then learn the song by watching your teacher play it.

Some songs come with a picture. The rest are waiting for you to make up a story, choose a name, and draw a picture for them.

Have fun!

Owl Song

Moderato

O - wl   sits   and   o - wl   flies.
Hoo   hoo   haa   haa   hoo   hoo   haa!

O - wl   sings   songs   at   mid - night.
Hoo   hoo   haa   haa   hoo   hoo   haa!

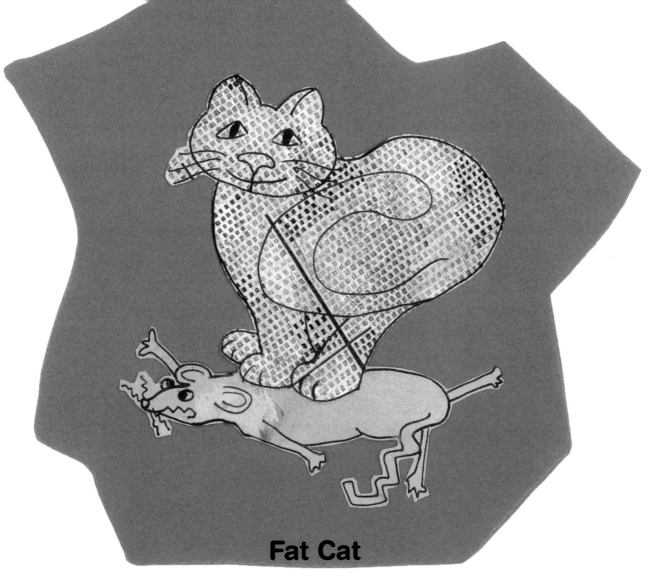

Fat Cat

Moderato

Fat   cat   fat fat   cat.   Fat   cat   saw   a   rat.

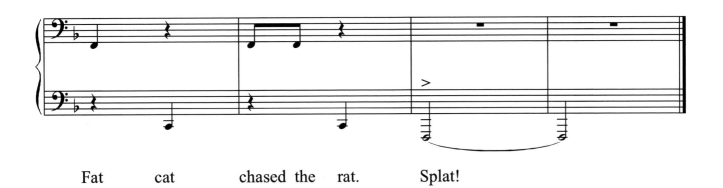

Fat   cat   chased the   rat.   Splat!

54

Allegro

Children's Song

Vivace

Mahoor, Tune by Ataollah Khoram

Black Keys

Sam Kaplan-Pettus, age 5

I Can Read the Notes

Playing While Looking at the Notes
Dropping and Lifting on the Long Fingers

Here are some songs for you to start playing while looking at the notes. I am sure you will like most of them, but you don't have to play them all.

Choose many of them to practice playing non-legato and staccato with relaxed wrists. You can come back to the rest of the pieces later and sight-read them.

Some songs have dynamic signs. The rest are waiting for you to decide how loudly or softly they should be played based on the story that you make.

Enjoy!

60

Going Up, Going Down

Russian Folk Song

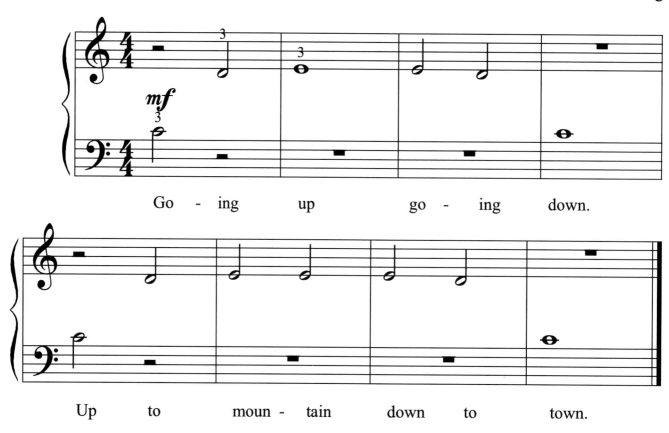

Go - ing   up   go - ing   down.

Up   to   moun - tain   down   to   town.

Russian Folk Song

62

Russian Folk Song

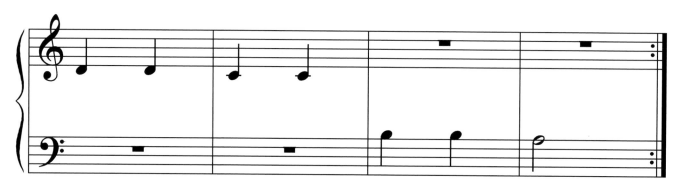

Russian Children's Song

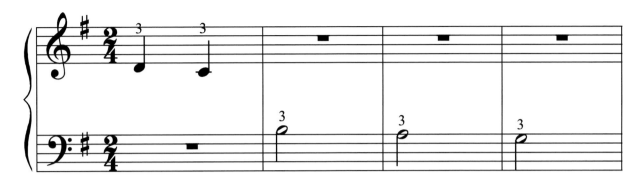

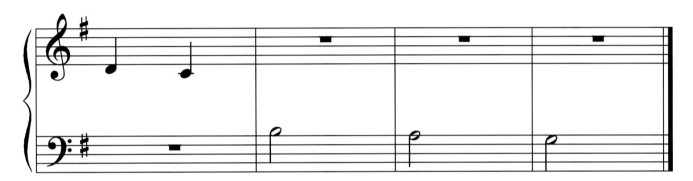

64

Folk Song

Iranian Children's Song

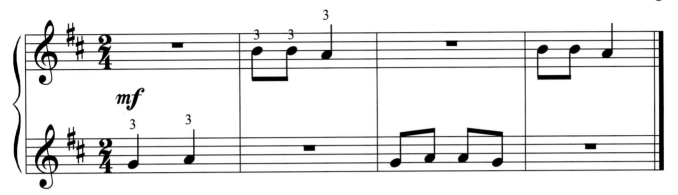

Iranian Folk Song

Folk Song

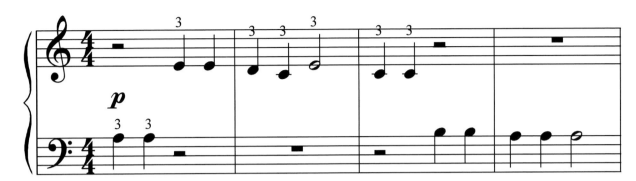

Twinkle Twinkle Little Star

Folk Song

Two Happy Geese

Russian Folk Song

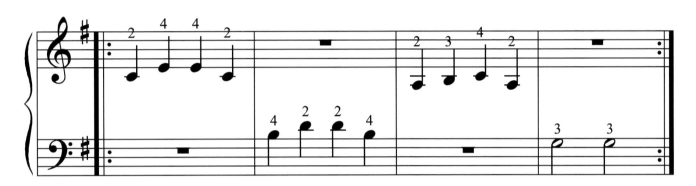

Tatar Folk Song

Playing In The Snow

Tune by Samin Bagnolesi

Russian Folk Song

Running

Nicolas Theunissen, age 8

Allegro

Geraman Folk Song

Moderato

My Fingers Can Sing

Legato Playing

Here are some pieces to practice playing legato. Choose a bunch of them that you like the best and teach your fingers how to sing on the piano with beautiful, smoothly connected sounds.

Some songs have tempo marks. The rest are waiting for you to decide how fast or slow they should be played based on the story that you make.

Why don't you review the songs that you have learned so far in this book and choose a tempo mark for each of them.

Have fun practicing!

Étude

Elena Gnessina

The Doll

Moderato cantabile

Tune by Samin Baghtcheban

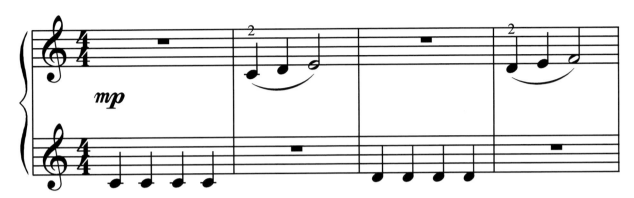

The Rainbow

Moderato

Azal Laal, age 5

82

Iranian Folk Song

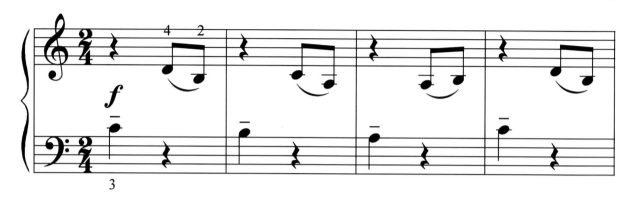

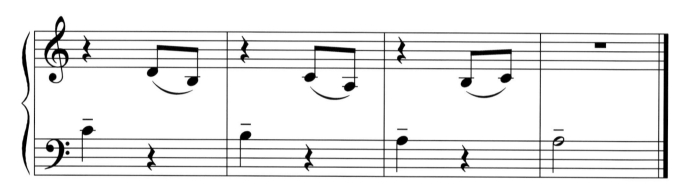

Iranian Folk Song

My Beautiful Train

Allegretto

Tune by Samin Baghtcheban

London Bridge

Moderato

Folk Song

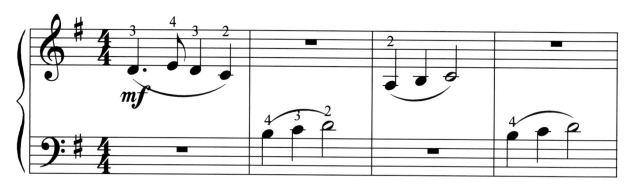

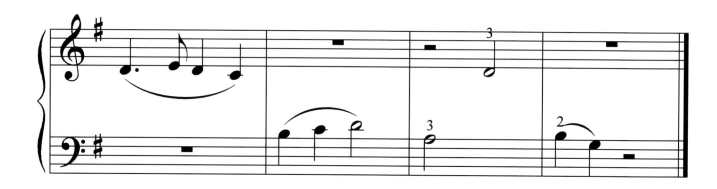

Folk Song

Doll's Lullaby

Andante cantabile

Tune by Samin Baghtcheban

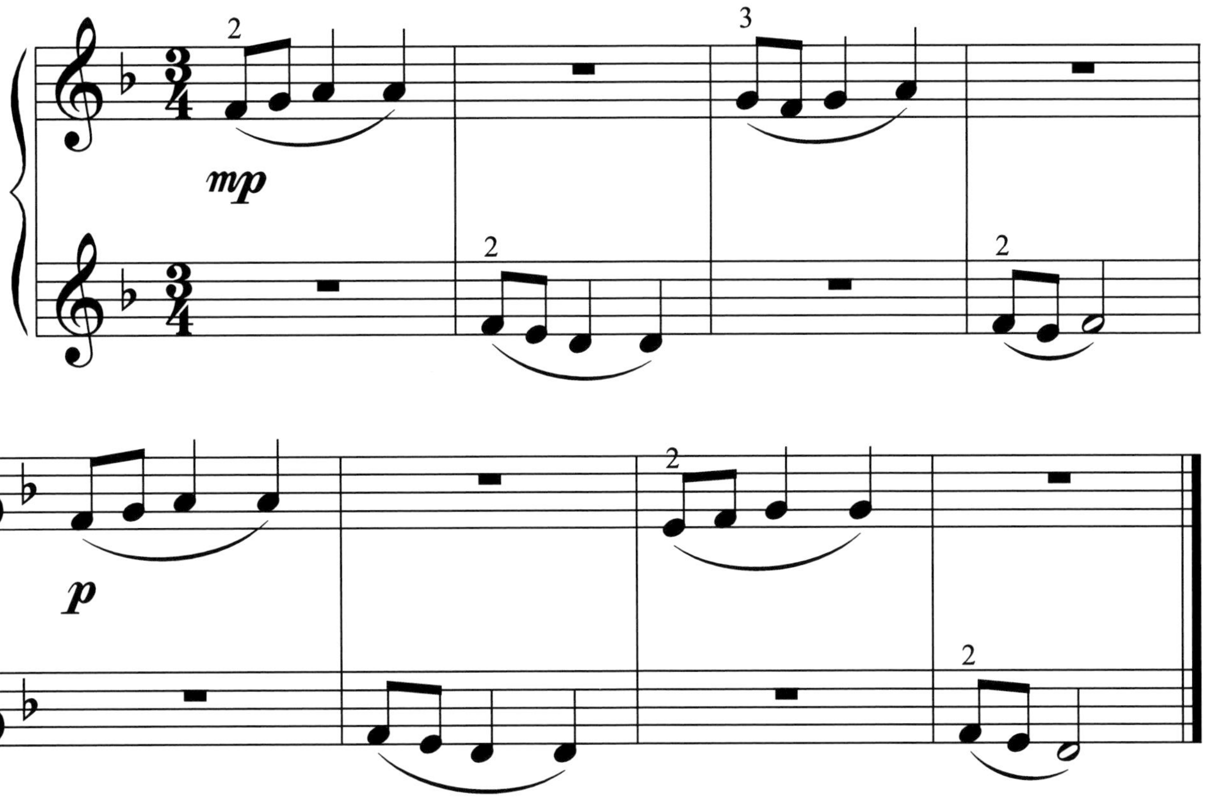

Italian Folk Song

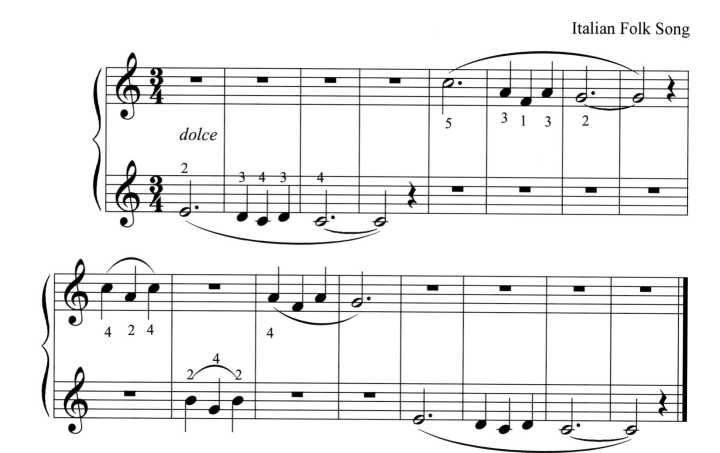

Ukrainian Folk Song

92

Cantabile

Iranian Folk Song

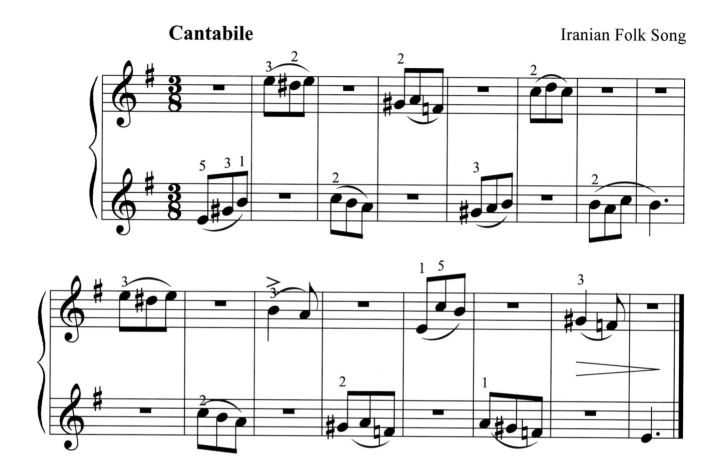

Cantabile

Ukrainian Folk Song

The Snake

Allegro moderato

Iranian Folk Song

Andante

Folk Song

Allegretto

Iranian

Adagio

Iranian Folk Song

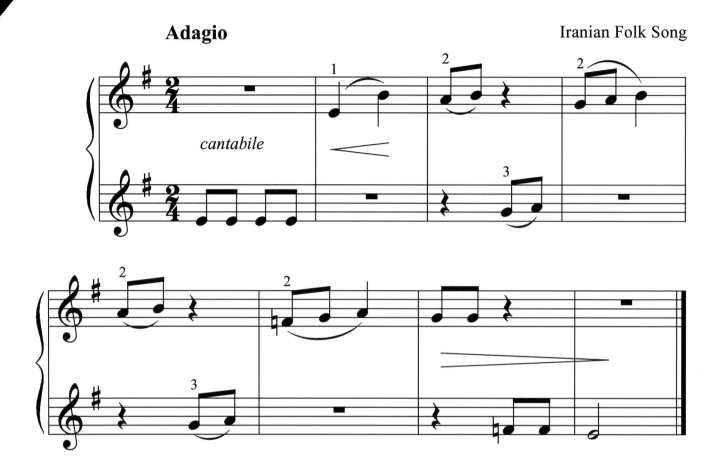

cantabile

Iranian Folk Song

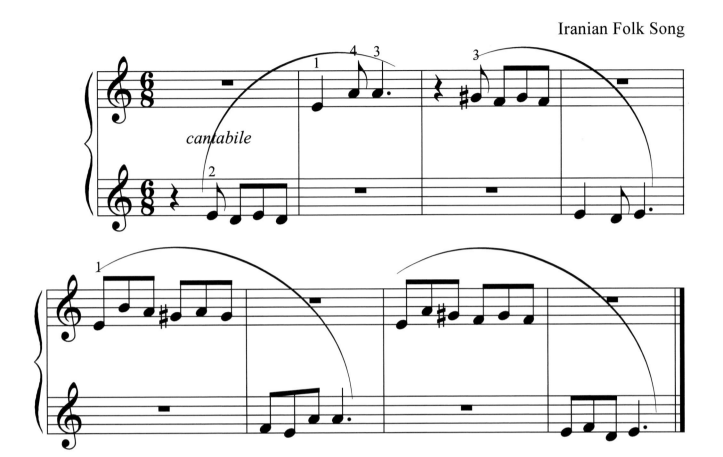

Russian Folk Song

Andante cantabile

Iranian Folk Song

legato

Haunted House

Andante

Sam Kaplan-Pettus, age 5

I Can Play with Both Hands at the Same Time

Playing Pieces with Melody and Accompaniment
Polyphonic Pieces

Doing two different things at the same time with each hand is not easy. You need to make sure that your melody is singing and your accompaniment is quiet. Choose many of these pieces and master them, listening to each hand very carefully.

Some of these pieces were written by other students. Have you ever tried to make your own music? It is quite fun!

Cantabile

Russian Folk Song

Moderato

Belarusian Folk Song

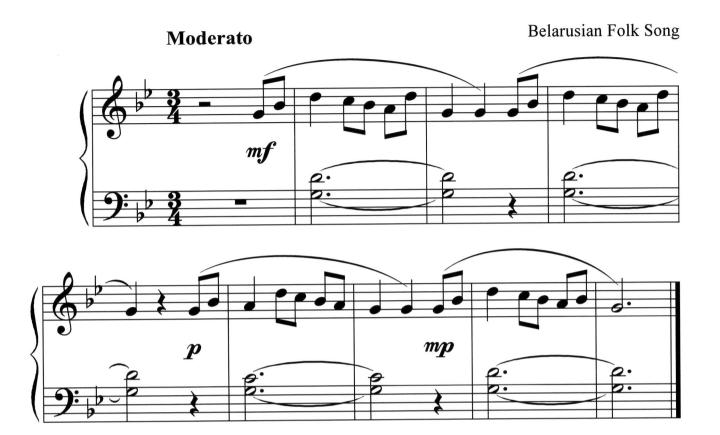

108

Allegro moderato

Russian Folk Song

Allegro

Iranian Folk Song

Moderato

Iranian Folk Song

Andante

Armenian Folk Song

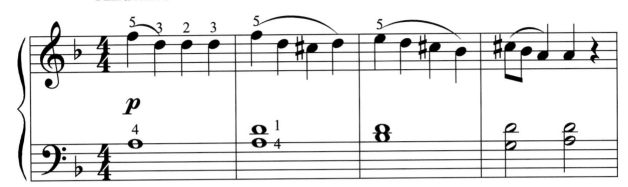

Cantabile

Russian Folk Song

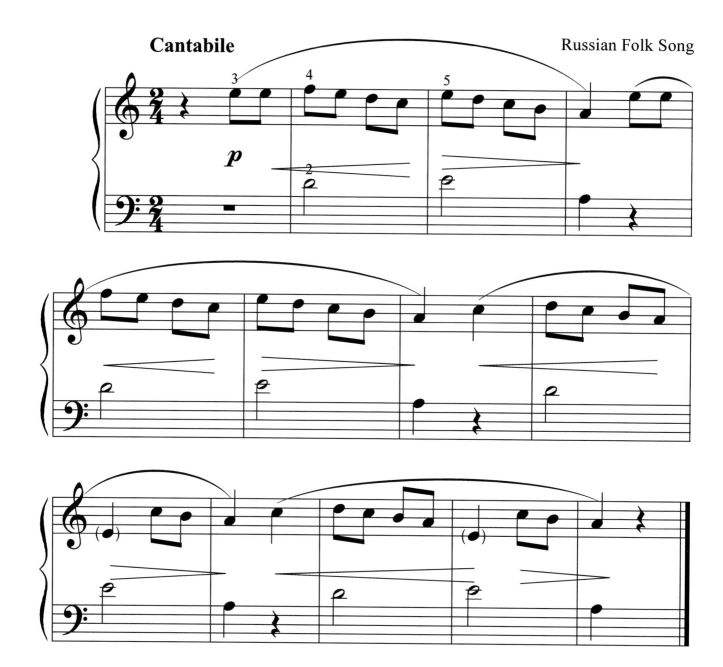

Andante Russian Folk Song

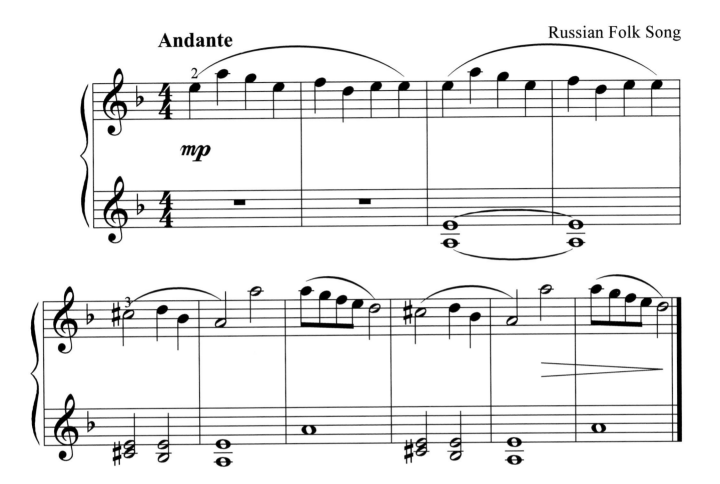

Iranian Folk Song

Lento

Tune by Samin Baghtcheban

Con moto

Iranian Folk Song

118

Allegretto

Allegretto

Iranian Folk Song

120

Cantabile

Iranian Folk Song

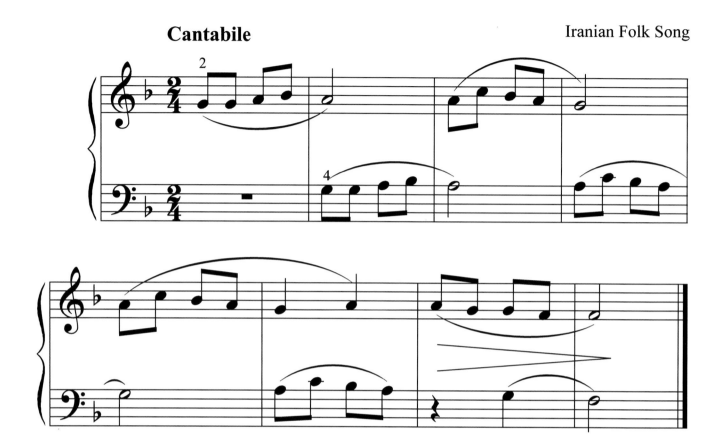

The Mommy Cat

Tune by Samin Baghtcheban

Moderato

The Mommy Cat

Moderato

Tune by Samin Baghtcheban

Bears Wobbling

Nikolas Nettesheim, age 6

124

Moderato

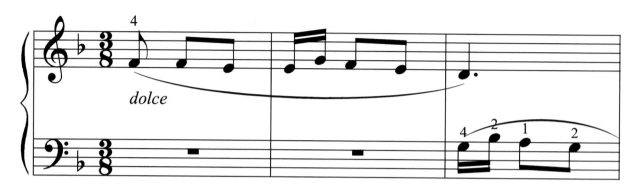

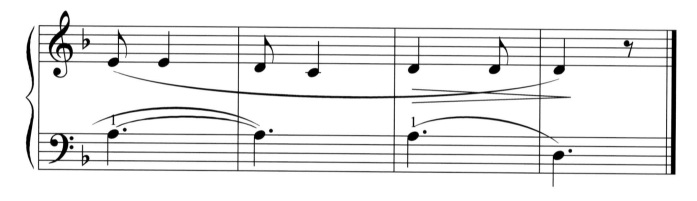

Allegro moderato

Mexican Folk Song

I Can Play More Fun Music

Playing Pieces with More Diverse Accompaniment
More Polyphonic Pieces

Now it is time to master more interesting pieces. Some of these pieces can be played with the pedal. The pedal will change the color of the sound. Notice how the sound changes when you use the pedal and decide where to use it in each piece.

Good luck!

The Playful Pony

Allegro moderato

Tune by Samin Baghtcheban

Moderato

Iranian Folk Song

legato

Espressivo

Iranian Folk Song

Moderato

Tune by Samin Baghtcheban

Grazioso

Iranian Folk Song

Practice
1. Separate
2. SLOW!

Grazioso

Iranian Folk Song

134

Con moto

Iranian Folk Song

This Is A Funny Way To Dance

Tempo di valse

Elaine Jutamulia, age 6

This Is Our Garden

Con brio

Tune by Samin Baghtcheban

Where The Deer Lives

Spiritoso

Tune by Samin Baghtcheban

Grazioso

Russian Folk Song

My Vocabulary Sheet

Music Terms That I Know

01   f   forte   loud

02   p   piano   soft

03   mf   mezzo forte   medium loud

04   mp

05   Allegro

06   Moderato

07   Andante

08

09

10

11

12

13

14

15

16 _____

17 _____

18 _____

19 _____

20 _____

21 _____

22 _____

23 _____

24 _____

25 _____

26 _____

27 _____

28 _____

29 _____

30 _____

МИНИСТЕРСТВО КУЛЬТУРЫ РОССИЙСКОЙ ФЕДЕРАЦИИ

ГОСУДАРСТВЕННЫЙ МУЗЫКАЛЬНЫЙ КОЛЛЕДЖ имени ГНЕСИНЫХ

121069, Москва, ул. Поварская, д. 38, стр. 1, Тел. 691-3855   Факс. 691-3102

Every musician, especially a teacher, undergoes a long way of training and absorbs the achievements of different musicians, to whom he listens and with whom he consorts. However, when the musician starts the teaching process, it is never just a recurrence; it is always a new experience. A Thousand Stories for a Little Pianist by Katrin Arefy, a graduate of the State Musical College named after Gnessins, is both traditional and innovative.

The methodical traditions have their origin in the Russian schools of H. Neuhaus, E. Gnessina, T. Yudovina-Galperina, but mostly in the school of A. Artobolevskaya. The novelty lies in the selection of the material, in the choice of children's repertoire, and in the skillful combination of classical and folk music in the tactful and keen arrangements of Katrin Arefy.

The main idea is that every child is talented and unique, but the musical atmosphere is very important for his development, and this factor becomes decisive.

Practicing based on this method will certainly be useful for children, will broaden their range of vision and bring them into the magical world of music.

Honored Figure of Culture of Russia
Member of European Piano Teachers Association – EPTA
Member of International Association "Art & Education"
Irina Temchenko

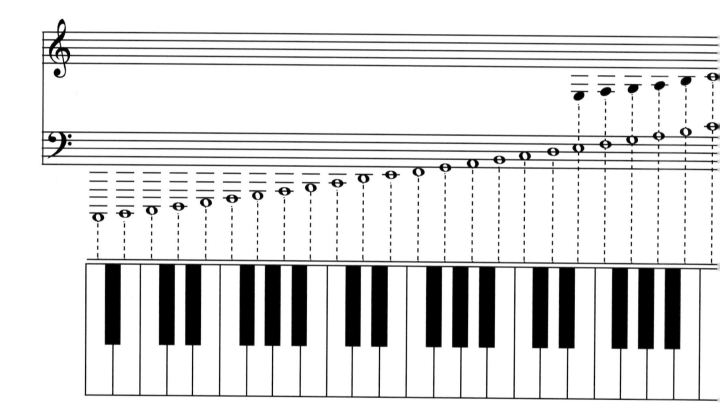

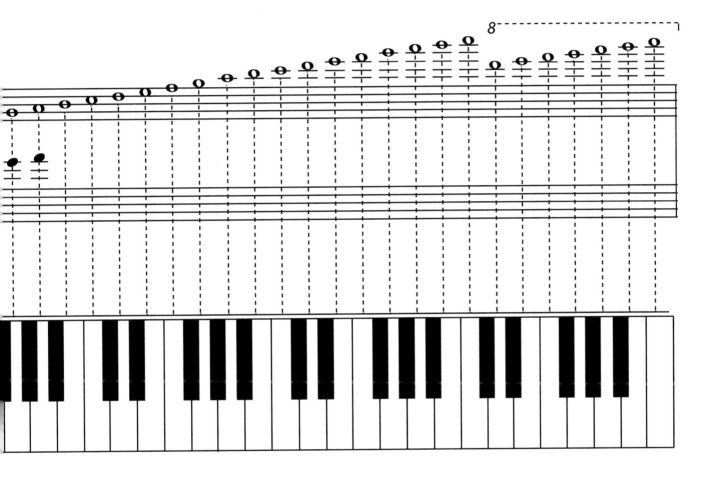